Taking Action

Anti-Bias Learning: Social Justice in Action

By Emily Chiariello

21st Century
Junior Library

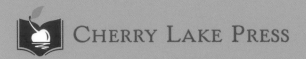

Published in the United States of America by Cherry Lake Publishing Group
Ann Arbor, Michigan
www.cherrylakepublishing.com

Developed with help from Learning for Justice, a project of the Southern Poverty Law Center. With special thanks to Monita Bell and Hoyt Phillips.
Reading Adviser: Beth Walker Gambro, MS, Ed., Reading Consultant, Yorkville, IL

Photo Credits: © Rawpixel.com/Shutterstock.com, cover, 1; © Ira Bostic/Shutterstock.com, 4; © hxdbzxy/ Shutterstock.com, 6; © GagliardiPhotography/ Shutterstock.com, 8; © Stock Rocket/Shutterstock.com, 10; © Creativa Images/Shutterstock.com, 12; © Monkey Business Images/Shutterstock.com, 14, 20; © 4 PM production/Shutterstock.com, 16; © Diego Cervo/Shutterstock.com, 18

Cherry Lake Press is an imprint of Cherry Lake Publishing Group.

Library of Congress Cataloging-in-Publication Data has been filed and is available at catalog.loc.gov

Cherry Lake Publishing Group would like to acknowledge the work of the Partnership for 21st Century Learning, a Network of Battelle for Kids. Please visit http://www.battelleforkids.org/networks/p21 for more information.

Printed in the United States of America
Corporate Graphics

CONTENTS

Taking social action can be big, like going to a protest,
or small, like speaking up for a friend.

I Care

I care about how people are treated.

Did you know you have power? Even though it might not always feel that way, you have the power to make changes and solve problems.

When we take **social action**, we act in a way that makes the world a better place.

Feelings lead to actions. If we feel cold, we can put on a jacket. If we feel bored, we can read a book.

Finding a spot to sit in the lunchroom can be scary for some.
Think about a time you've been nervous at school.

When we take social action, it's usually because we have feelings of care or concern. We pay attention to how people, including ourselves, are treated. We don't want to be treated unfairly, and we feel bad when other people are treated unfairly.

Sunny noticed that one of her classmates, Russell, always sits alone at lunch. She asked her friend Valerie if she knows why. "He's gross!" Valerie replied. "His family is super poor, and he's always coughing."

But Sunny knows it's not fair to **exclude** Russell just because his family doesn't have much money. Russell is being treated unfairly. Thinking about Russell makes Sunny feel sad. She's concerned about his feelings.

School is one place you may need to address unfairness.
Where else might you see unfairness?

I Am Responsible

I know it's important to stand up for myself and others.

Have you ever been in a situation like Sunny, when you have a feeling that something is not right? How do you decide what to do? Should you act? Or should you just let things be the way they are?

We each have a **responsibility** to do something when we see **injustice** or unfairness. Sometimes, this means speaking up for ourselves or for others.

A trusted adult can help you speak up when you see injustice.

And sometimes, we need help from other people, like adults, to find our power to do this.

Sunny decided to ask her mom for advice about how she can speak up for Russell.

Think!

What actions can you take to make your home, school, and community better places?

Speaking up for yourself and others doesn't have to be loud.
Sometimes, quiet words can have a big impact.

Speaking Up!

I speak up with courage when something is unfair.

You can take different kinds of actions when someone is being hurtful or something is unfair. One of the most powerful things you can do is use your voice to speak up.

It's important that when you speak up that you do it with respect, even if you disagree with someone's words or behavior.

Talking with friends about unfairness might feel hard—but friends should listen to each other with open minds.

Even though Valerie is her friend, Sunny disagreed with the way she treated Russell. With her mom's **encouragement**, Sunny decided to say something to Valerie.

"You shouldn't be so mean to him, Valerie," Sunny said. "You don't know what Russell's life is like. It's not fair to treat him badly because of his family's **income**."

Create!

Make posters celebrating people for being brave and speaking up for what is right. Decorate your classroom or school hallways with the posters.

You can take action against injustice with your voice and the choices you make—like who you sit with on the bus.

Making Choices

I take action if I see unfairness, even when it's hard to do.

Speaking up is a really important step in taking action. But what happens next? How do we create change?

In addition to speaking up with our voices, we can make new choices and behave in different ways to bring about more fairness.

That's what Valerie did after Sunny talked to her. "Maybe you're right," Valerie said. "I'm sure it makes him feel terrible. I ride the bus with Russell. I can try to get to know him better."

When we all work together, we can accomplish great things.

Working Together

I work with others to make our community fair for everyone.

When we work together with our friends, family, and community, we can be even more powerful than when we do things alone. Great things can happen when groups of people work hard and **cooperate** to achieve a goal.

The most powerful kinds of social action happen when groups of people plan creative ways to make the world fairer for everyone.

Being a friend is a great start to making the world fairer.

After Sunny spoke up, Valerie started treating Russell kindly and with more respect. Then Valerie and Sunny asked Russell to eat with them at lunch. Soon, two other classmates joined. Russell felt more included, and everyone got to hang out with some new friends.

How can you take action to make the world fairer?

Ask Questions!

What's something you would like to do to make the world a better place? What help do you need? What questions do you have? Talk to an adult or older kid to get new ideas about how you can take action.

GLOSSARY

cooperate (koh-AH-puh-rayt) to work together toward a goal

encouragement (in-KUHR-ij-muhnt) the act of being kind and supportive to someone

exclude (ik-SKLOOD) to keep someone from joining or taking part

income (IN-kuhm) money that someone earns

injustice (in-JUH-stuhss) unfair treatment

responsibility (ri-spahn-suh-BIH-luh-tee) a duty or job

social action (SOH-shuhl AK-shuhn) actions taken by people to improve life for everyone

FIND OUT MORE

WEBSITES

Learning for Justice Classroom Resources—Students texts, tasks, and more
https://www.learningforjustice.org/classroom-resources

Learning for Justice—Learn more about anti-bias work and find the full Social Justice Standards framework
https://www.learningforjustice.org

Social Justice Books—Booklists and a guide for selecting anti-bias children's books
https://socialjusticebooks.org

Welcoming Schools—Creating safe and welcoming schools
https://www.welcomingschools.org

INDEX

ABOUT THE AUTHOR

Emily Chiariello is an anti-bias educator, educational consultant, and former classroom teacher. She is the principal author of the Learning for Justice Social Justice Standards. Emily lives in Buffalo, New York.